The Stations of the Cross
INRI
Accompanying Jesus on His Way to Calvary
I0797520

Jesus, You have united heaven and earth through the sacrifice of Your body and blood upon the cross. You have brought all those who believe in You to God, the Father. Help me to think often about what You did for my salvation and the salvation of the whole world.

Jesus, our Lord, stands before Pilate having been brought there by the religious leaders. Just days before, He had been praised by the people of the city, and now He stands before the governor, accused of many things. Pilate questions Him, and Jesus remains silent. The crowds call out for His death, and still our Lord is silent. Pilate, wanting to please the crowd, condemns our Lord to death.

Having been whipped, beaten, and made fun of, Jesus is humiliated even further by being made to carry the cross on which He is to die. Weak and in pain from all that has been inflicted upon Him, our Lord takes up His cross. It is very heavy, but not as heavy as the weight of our sins. Then He is led to the Place of the Skull, which in Hebrew is called Golgotha, to be put to death.

How difficult it must have been to carry the heavy weight of the cross upon shoulders that had been whipped and torn. As Jesus begins His journey to the place of execution, He makes His way through the city. Some people weep and others yell out insults. Suffering and exhausted, our Lord falls under the weight of the cross.

Rising once again, Jesus slowly makes His way through the narrow streets suffering in silence—suffering alone—until He looks up and sees a face among the multitude. It is a face streaming with tears. It is His mother. Brokenhearted, she approaches Him. She cannot stop what is happening, but Mary can share His sorrow.

Jesus falters in His steps. The Roman soldiers are impatient. They pull an onlooker from the crowd and force him to help Jesus carry the cross. The man's name is Simon and he is from Cyrene. Little does he know he is helping his own Savior and Lord.

Every painful step takes Jesus closer to the edge of the city where He will suffer a cruel death. The agony is made more difficult by the insults He bears along the way. Then, from the crowd, a woman steps out. With great love, she wipes Jesus' face with a cloth. It is a moment of relief for our Lord. Miraculously, the image of His face remains on the fabric—a reminder of the love that drove Him to the cross for our salvation.

The road to Golgotha is a difficult one and once again Jesus falls. The soldiers demand He rise again, and some of the people in the crowd are appalled by the way Jesus is treated. Others simply jeer at Him again. Slowly Jesus rises to His feet. His gaze is ahead to where He will fulfill what He has come to do—bring us salvation. He continues His way, one painful step after the other.

As Jesus makes His way to the outskirts of the city, He is met by a group of women weeping at the sight of His suffering. Gazing upon them, Jesus tells them not to weep for Him but for those who do not recognize the work of God.

The place of His death is just ahead and the Lord struggles to reach it. He falls a third time. Once more He is forced to His feet and made to climb the hill where He, the Lamb of God, will take away the sins of the world.

Jesus has given everything. All that remains are the clothes He is wearing. In preparation for the crucifixion, they are taken off. Since His cloak has value, the soldiers throw dice for it, not realizing that the man that stands before them is of greater value than all creation. Jesus is silent, patient, and long-suffering.

Having reached the top of the hill, Jesus is made to lie on the cross. His arms are stretched out to both sides, His legs, to the foot of the cross. The soldiers take nails and crucify our Lord.

Having suffered on the cross for hours, the Lord cries out, "Father, into Your hands I commend My spirit!" Great darkness comes upon the land. In the temple the veil between the holy place and the holy of holies tears in two. Jesus has died.

While some abandon our Lord in the time of His suffering, others do not. Jesus is taken down from the cross. He is placed on His grieving mother's lap. He is wept over and He is mourned. The Son of God came as a helpless child, and now, He lies upon the same lap. He has done what He came to do.

A wealthy man named Joseph of Arimathea, a follower of our Lord, has obtained permission from Pilate to take the body and prepare it for burial. With loving care, the body of Jesus is wrapped in linen and laid in a tomb.